SPOTS OF TIME

Norman Bissett

Indigo Dreams Publishing

First Edition: Norman Bissett
First published in Great Britain in 2011 by:
Indigo Dreams Publishing
132 Hinckley Road
Stoney Stanton
Leicestershire
LE9 4LN

www.indigodreams.co.uk

ISBN 978-1-907401-64-0

British Library Cataloguing in Publication Data. A CIP record for this book can be obtained from the British Library.

Designed and typeset in Palatino Linotype by Indigo Dreams.

Cover design by Ronnie Goodyer at Indigo Dreams from a photograph by Matthew Bissett.

Printed and bound in Great Britain by Imprint Academic, Exeter.

For our Grandchildren,
Max and Kate

BORN TODAY

Born in the Simpson after being borne
like gold or myrrh or frankincense
from distant oases,
she shines, a star.
Today
is her birth day.
Worshippers gather round,
dumbfounded by this miracle of life,
borne from the East in order to be born.

Edinburgh, August 1st, 2011

Acknowledgements

Many of the poems in this collection have previously appeared, either in print or electronically, in such publications as Tips, E-Tips, Quantum Leap, First Time, Poetry Cornwall, Metverse Muse, Waves, Reach Poetry, Rubies in the Darkness, Author, Wavelengths, Weyfarer, FreeXpresSions, Orbis, Assent, the new writer, United Press Ltd, Forward Press, Aspire, The Interpreter's House and elsewhere.

Acknowledgements and thanks are due to the Editors of these publications. I am especially grateful to Wendy Webb for her friendship and unstinting support.

Previous Publications

Following The Wagons
A Potful Of Pansies
Quest For The Quetzal
The Ties That Bind
Langass: And Other Poems
The Makin' Green And Other Poems
Lanterns And Flowers
Piercing The Darkness
Gleanings
A Peedie Pot-Pourri
Painting The Bridge

CONTENTS

SPOTS OF TIME

There are in our existence spots of time
That with distinct pre-eminence retain
A renovating virtue, whence, depressed
By false opinion and contentious thought,
Or aught of heavier or more deadly weight,
In trivial occupations, and the round
Of ordinary intercourse, our minds
Are nourished and invisibly repaired;
A virtue, by which pleasure is enhanced,
That penetrates, enables us to mount,
When high, more high, and lifts us up when fallen.
...Such moments
Are scattered everywhere, taking their date
From our first childhood...

Wordsworth, *The Prelude*, Book XII

A LANDSCAPE OF PEARLS

Week after week the skies were full
of blizzards sent to try us. Untrodden snow
lay two feet deep. Trees in their nakedness
huddled beneath white counterpanes.
Robins and blue tits froze on black boughs.

Paralysed beneath its ermine covering,
our pewter canal stretched to the horizon,
an iron pathway prophesying doom.
Gales from Alaska and the Caucasus
swept over us, howling in Cyrillic—

before subsiding. Eventually, blown out,
they passed away, slumping to the ground,
chap-fallen. Small birds, survivors, reappeared,
reclaiming eaves and chimney tops.
Exhausted drifts sank down into the earth.

Throughout the land, the fight back
has begun. Beneath the azaleas,
two dozen mitred daffodils thrust upwards
through the soil, spearsmen contesting
Bannockburn and Stirling Bridge. Snowdrops salute

more temperate skies at Dundas Castle
and Dalmeny House. The woods at Annandale,
festooned with pearls, extend to Dora's Field
and both banks of the Ouse. Bedecked in delicate green
and drooping white, Norfolk celebrates.

I must arise and go now and make a pilgrimage
to Walsingham, to the Holy House
of golden stone, to our Lady's shrine,
there to give thanks for some two thousand years
of snowdrops and their resurrection.

I'll cross the bridge to the little woodland dell
close to the ruined priory, just after dawn, as the sun comes up.
I'll genuflect with reverence, in gratitude
to the old lady whose lifetime work of love it was
to plant these bulbs and create a landscape of pearls.

ALL THINGS BRIGHT AND BEAUTIFUL

Hovering rainbows,
humming-birds at Iguazú
soar from the palette.

We stand on a rock
at the lip of the cauldron,
semi-hypnotized.

ADAGIETTO

Maestosamente
on its slow, sedate passage,
the pleasure steamer

proceeds at three knots
beyond the *Arsenale*
to the Grand Canal.

A harp balances
the shimmering violins'
soft, heart-breaking thrum,

the *adagio*
evoking (*lentamente)*
mirage-like beauty

and a perfection
that is unattainable.
On the polluted

beach of the Lido,
Von Aschenbach sits weeping.
His mascara runs,

black pomade trickling
slowly down waxen features,
disintegrating.

AHEAD OF US

Ahead of us,
a plump young lass
and, at the front of the queue,
a frail old woman
standing
with two partly-filled,
plastic bags,
waiting
in the ice-cold wind-tunnel
for the number twenty seven.

Ahead of us,
at the front of the queue,
a sudden flurry of consternation,
a minor commotion.
The old woman is down,
slumped, crumpled at the foot of the bus stop,
her frail cheek
pressed hard against the soft slush,
her plastic bags scattering gewgaws and green beans
across the pavement.

The plump young lass,
quickest on the uptake,
dashes into the sushi place adjacent
to the bus stop
to phone for an ambulance.
Next in line,
my wife and I
lift up the frail old lady.
She is as insubstantial
as a half-filled bag of bones.

We prop her against murky December glass,
holding her secure
on the edge of the four inch plastic bench
of the windy bus shelter.
We wipe cold slush
from her parchment-coloured cheek,
brush snow
from her raincoat,
gather up her scattered knick-knacks,
lentils and a loaf of bread.

Her cheeks are ashen, jaundiced,
drained of blood,
whiter than dry ice.
Her eyelids flicker, seeking closure.
We speak her awake
but she drifts in and out of consciousness,
threatening once more to slump
towards the eternal cold.
We prop her up, prevent her pitching
downwards into the tantalising slush.

A kindly, considerate Japanese
invites us in to the warmth of his sushi place,
heady with monosodium glutamate
and prawn teriyaki.
We carry her inside
and set her down on an upholstered bench,
book-ended between plastic bags.
We bring her green tea
but she is too weak
to raise the bowl-sized cup.
The ambulance arrives.

Two paramedics dressed in green
like mediaeval vegetation gods
materialise, bearing equipment.
I brief them over a mini-Alp. They nod, all competence.
They step inside. And all is well.
Several buses
have come and gone.
We are now at the front of the queue,

standing
in the ice-cold wind tunnel,
waiting
for the number twenty seven.

ALCHEMY

From Damascus,
through Deraa and Jerash
we drove
from the Dead Sea
via Jericho
up to Jerusalem.

We arrived
at dusk
just as the setting sun
touched the Dome of the Rock,
creating an arc of gold
like the dawn of creation.

AND HERONS LIKE SENTINELS

Such wonders we have seen this week—
The Night Watch
and *The Kitchen Maid*—
such prodigies of light and shade,
serenely peaceful Dutch interiors.

We have celebrated domestic stability
in *The Yellow House at Arles,*
have smelt irises and almond blossom,
and felt the dread of crows, like vultures,
flapping, tormented, above a field of wheat.

Have sat in the Concertgebouw
and heard electrifying music,
the stunning, plangent coup de théâtre
of Dvořák's opening chords,
played by the world's best orchestra.

Yet, strangely, what endures
amidst the art and architecture, music and canals
is the pullulating bird-life, the communities
of geese, ducks, moorhens, coots and swans,
infesting Waterworld and the grasslands of East Friesia.

ANGKOR WAT

Colossal faces
decaying into the trees
watch us, like Buddha.

APPEASEMENT

The world is sleeping
following its long battle
of the night before.
The wind has ceased to attack.
Grey sky. Continuing snow.

This uneasy truce
will probably be broken.
There is more to come.
It is doubtless premature
to proclaim peace in our time.

AUGURIES

Autumn.
September gone.
Leaves accumulating
by the roadside. An air of
sadness.

Christmas
is threatening.
At Aberlady Bay,
skeins of wild geese are touching down
once more.

Hedgerows
lining the road
that leads to Logan Lea
yield up wizened rose-hips and dead
rowans.

AUTOLYCUS

'Put your hands together,'
orders my grandson
with all the savoir faire
and confident
omniscience
of a two-year old
as he mis-tosses
his ball backwards
over his head
then chases it,
like Mercury.

I who for years
fielded at first slip,
crouching tiger-like,
with an eagle's eye,
a snapper-up
of unconsidered trifles,
the scourge of waywardness,
a scooper-up of snicks,
now find it hard to stoop.
Upright, I'll coach him
in the art of spinning.

BARCELONA

That you are enthused
by Barcelona,
our old stomping ground,
does not surprise us.
We share your delight.

When you get back, let
us trade impressions,
swap experiences,
exchange our findings,
new and not so new.

BATTLE OF THE SCALES

Fat Freddie who hailed from Dumfries
was concerned about looking obese.
Umpteen trips to the gym
made scant difference to him
till he drowned in a puddle of grease.

BAUDELAIRE'S REVERIE

Greedy, indeed, in voluptuous headiness,
have you never inhaled the powerful bouquet
of a grain of incense percolating through a church,
breathed in the potency of musk in a sachet?

Mysterious necromancy by which the resurrected past
conjures the here and now, the eternal present.
Thus the lover gathers up the exquisite flower
of memory from the beloved's body's scent,

from the potent, palpable sachet gathers it up,
her censer of heavy, coiled, cascading hair, beauty
from which the wild musk rises up,

as from her fabrics—silk, muslin, velvet—
each permeated with her youthful purity,
there emanates the perfume of her skin.

Forest and desert, sun and swaying billow
perfume her coiled, cascading, golden hair.
Her head upon my perfumed pillow,
as enigmatic as the Sphinx, lies there.

As from a censer rich with musk
fragrance pervades her youthful skin.
She coils, hypnotic as the dusk,
shadowy, warm and palpable as sin.

BENEATH THE WATERS

Although this February day is dank
and the ditches all muddy with snow-melt,
the air is balmy and the wind silent,
svelte wavelets lapping gently upon stones.

Across the reservoir I hear the cackling gulls,
the chattering of magpies and strident rooks.
Two sloe-black cormorants like caryatids
on the Erectheum perch on a ruined outcrop.

On his palfrey mounted, the Bruce surveyed
from Kirkton Hill the outcome of a bet.
One knight, the audacious William St Clair,
had wagered his own life that his two hounds

would bring to earth a mystical white deer
before it leapt the burn, to sanctuary.
With inches to spare, the dogs succeeded.
The heathery bank ran purple with gore.

Beneath the waters of the reservoir,
St Catherine's Chapel slumbers in the dark.
The hub of life for a community,
hundreds had known the hardness of its pews,

contracted marriages, registered new lives.
Farm hands and maidservants had been hired,
rents and feu duties paid, debts settled,
assizes held, malefactors punished.

Beneath the pewter's cold inscrutability,
Glencorse's murky shadows have submerged
the ruined chapel and the mystical white deer.
Two sloe-black cormorants like caryatids stand guard.

BEYOND CARING

Hunched in his wheelchair,
deaf aid turned down low,
he remembers the scrambled,
pre-dawn Hurricanes and Spitfires,

dog-fights over Winchelsea and Rye,
the reverberating echoes of a castle door,
the Obergruppenfűhrer's wintry smile.
He re-enacts a perilous escape.

With a warm, damp face-cloth, Cathy,
his youthful carer, gently wipes
the grizzled cheeks and purple lips
and draws a comb through silvery wisps.

Colditz means nothing to her,
nor Stalag Luft III.
Per Ardua ad Astra is a foreign tongue,
like Esperanto. Possibly double Dutch.

The society beauty who drove
legions of suitors to drink or suicide,
with tremulous, feeble fingers spills her tea
and scatters digestive biscuit on the floor.

A one-time concert pianist of renown,
now she is bed-ridden, semi-paralysed.
Abandoning unsyncopated limbs,
Rachmaninov, Liszt and Grieg have fled away.

Her smiling, youthful carer, Dan, a devotee
of rhythm and blues, coaxes her patiently
to try the soup. Today, it is ham and pea.
The green abomination trickles down her chin.

BLEAK MOUNTAIN

A convivial lunch
beside the Falls.
A short, agreeable

stroll into Banchory.
As twilight gathered,
we drove home

over Cairn o'Mount.
You returned to
an empty house.

BLESS RELAXES

In a straitjacket,
implacable leather straps
exercise restraint.
A lattice of bandages
prevents the limbs from moving.

In a chrysalis,
new life forms. A butterfly
emerges, crêpe-winged.
It unfurls rainbow colours
to celebrate its freedom.

BLIND

Deprived of all light,
she illuminates the world
with her inner glow.

BLOCKING THE BASILICA

I stumbled once
upon a notorious
American Beat Poet,

hirsute and Buddhaesque,
occupying the topmost
step in Montmartre.

His considerable bulk
obstructed my view
of Sacré Coeur.

BOOK OF BOOKS

Fully committed, eloquent,
passionate and erudite,
he addressed us

in Knox's church,
from Knox's pulpit,
with palpable convict ion.

It was remarkable—
a popular celebrity
professing sincere belief.

BOOM AND BUST

Great heaps of gold pile up in the gutter,
cascading from the trees—
sycamore, chestnut, beech, ash—
an abundance of sheer treasure.
The cart passes, brushes whirling,
and the gold disappears.

BORA BORA

Returning next day,
we purchased tiles,
ceramics, a kilim,

avoiding the Grand
Bazaar's inevitable hassle.
We particularly liked

the shop's quietude,
quality, atmosphere, prices
and hoş geldiniz,

but, above all,
the mutual respect
and obvious friendship

between the owner
and his colleague.
Both were elderly,

white-haired, infirm,
the one Turkish,
the other Armenian.

BOROBUDUR

Seven
terraces, four
square and three circular—
spiritual enlightenment
in stone

rising
through different
levels in the middle
of Java: a stepped pyramid.
Reliefs

below
delineate
common-or-garden sins,
bog standard crimes and punishments
for theft,

murder,
adultery—
a Dante-esque vision
of our earthbound iniquities.
Upper

reliefs
follow the life
of the historical
Buddha through this imperfect world:
high birth,

princely
position, wealth,
renunciation and
eventual enlightenment.
Statues

depict
him teaching and
meditating, coaxing
fellow pilgrims to continue
towards

the realm
of the spirit.
Pure spirit occupies
the large domed shrine on the structure's
summit.

BRACKETS

Our Tigris and Euphrates,
River Dee and River Don,
hold the city in their arms,
one bustling with oil money,
one tranquil as Balgownie.

BUMMELZUG

'Run, Grandad, run,'
orders our two year old,
pushing me
out of a sleepy siding
on to the main
East Coast line
from King's Cross
to the Waverley.

Thomas the Tank Engine
he is not, pottering
between thatched villages,
dragging slow feet
from time to time
to stand and stare
at buttercups, daisies,
water meadows, cows.

Boiler fully charged
and roaring comfortably,
pistons pounding,
he is a limited-stop express,
a bullet train hurtling
full speed ahead towards
a distant terminus
that keeps receding.

His heels flash
intermittently like
satellites or lighthouses
as round and round
the dining room table
he races, twinkling feet
scarcely touching the ground.
'Choo-choo. Choo-choo.

Run, Grandad, run.'
South of St Albans
I begin to flag and
run out of steam,
tank dehydrated.
Couplings hold up
as far as Peterborough
where I drop out of service.

BY THE TWEED

On Scottish rivers,
ducks and drakes are commonplace
and mallards routine.

Today's visitors
are handsome new immigrants,
thrilling exotics:

eider-ducks, a teal,
two red-breasted mergansers
and a crested grebe.

CAMBERWELL BEAUTIES

They fluttered up from London Docks
to settle on the hollyhocks
that once embellished Walthamstow,
Watford and Statford-atte-Bowe.

Fritillaries no longer thrive
in Camberwell and Rotherhithe.
Nectar is scarce and they refuse
to hang about with Limehouse Blues.

CATCHING SKY FLAKES

The chubby hands
of a laughing
child reach out,

attempting to clasp
the bright colours
of a butterfly

and capture beauty
before it disintegrates,
dessicated as dust.

CENTIPEDE

Guzzling
Vat 69,
Jock wi' the monyfeet
attempts to welcome the New Year
dancing.

COLD FEET

Iceland is well-named.
No one was eager to see
Gullfoss Waterfall.
Our group remained on the bus,
chatting about Florida.

CHRISTCHURCH

We giggled as we scattered bread
that day, basking in sunshine
on the grassy bank of an archetypal
English stream, flowing languorously

through what might have been
Winchester or Salisbury, any
royalist, High Tory, Home Counties town,
ducks quacking in an Oxford accent.

Was our journey of ten thousand miles
strictly necessary? We might have stayed
at home and fed the ducks on the canal,
from our bedroom window, without getting up.

We strolled into the unbroken peace
of the Cathedral, smaller than York or Lincoln,
Gloucester or Wells but cast in the same mould,
tranquillity reinforced by Handel's *Largo,* taped.

Now, in the twinkling of an eye,
that peace is shattered and the Cathedral
stands in ruins, spire, like the Campanile, collapsed
to rubble, shattered rose windows staining

the heaving ground. The sleepy, oh-so English
stream becomes a maelstrom, a tsunami wrenched
sloshing out of its disintegrating bed, flooding
each bank. Squattering ducks rise up and flee.

COFFEE STOP, ASSYNT

We sit in front of the Elphin Tea Rooms
at a glistening, rain-damp picnic bench
and raise a toast to Achiltibuie.
The whitewashed wall behind us is adorned
with antlers and wagon wheels with red spokes.
Looming in front of us, wreathed in Scotch mist,
four antediluvian pachyderms,
denizens since time immemorial,
squat on the skyline beyond peat-black bogs.
Cul Beag, Cul Mor, Suilven and Canisp slouch
through eternity, their skulls among clouds,
indifferent to sun, sleet, wind and snow.
Their granite flanks are perdurable.
Aristocrats, they lounge, lords of the land.

COUSIN NANCY

Beauty was married
to an intelligence rare
in our family.
I am grateful that we walked
to Lochnagar that summer.

CREMATION

The Lord's My Shepherd,
with cigarettes to follow
and chilled Chardonnay.

CROSSING THE CHARLES BRIDGE

The Vltava swirls.
We break stride to listen to
great Dixieland jazz.

CUZCO

Eccentric stones fit
together, jigsaw-fashion,
close as razor blades.

DECLINE

The birds are leaving,
nightjar, whinchat, red kite, swift.
They will not return,
corncrake and capercaillie
approaching oblivion.

A hundred thousand
unmapped seamounts are at risk
from deep-sea trawlers
which scrape summits, destroying
corals and Jurassic shrimps.

DAMSELFLY

Its broomstick body
bedazzles with stripes and spots.
Patrolling lakesides

and margins of ponds,
it darts hither and thither
on gossamer wings,

blue, whirring, gauze-like,
in a figure of eight blur.
A helicopter

looping and turning,
it flies sideways and backwards
skimming the surface

with agility,
characteristically
restless, electric.

Dragon eyes bulging,
it flashes iridescence,
like a kingfisher.

DEPENDENCE

The receiving line
at the Crematorium:
one father, one son.

DEMENTIA, WESTER ROSS

Out of the storm and into the foyer
he staggers, bewildered and slightly drunk.
His thin windcheater, obviously not
waterproof, is soaked across the shoulders
and even his shirt is wet. 'I don't know
where the bloody hell I am. Don't know
if this is a hotel. Where's my bloody room?
And where's my bloody wife?' He glowers around
the bus party, his fellow travellers,
cradling their Pimms and lagers by the fire.
Two rise and take his elbows. They murmur
reassuringly and try to calm down
terror masquerading as aggression.
Bowing his head, he stares into the abyss.

DESERT SONG

Eyes rimmed with kohl, arms heavy with golden
baubles and bangles from their own dowries,
ululating women fill the night sky
like peahens with skirling celebrations
as in their silken finery they greet
the arrival of the bride and groom.
Hypnotic oriental music throbs
on tabla, riq, oud, nay and kamanjah.
Ululation blends with undulation.
Two tables groan with dolma, patlican,
börek, fasulya, bamya, lahmajoon,
köfte, denderma, pilaf and plaki.
We should be in a yurt in Kurdestan
not David Lloyd's Sport Centre, Newhaven.

DISCOVERY

When winter leaves die,
the treasury is revealed:
a nest like a cup.

DISGUISED IN APPIN

Do not wear
full dress tartan
against a background

of bell heather
and rowan trees.
You will disappear,

camouflaged, chameleon-like,
by scarlet, green
and purple carbuncles.

EASYJET

They sit
in their frail tube
of aluminium,
as tightly packed as Havana
cigars.

They seem
oblivious
to winter's arrival.
The earth beneath them is hard, hoar
with frost.

DOLMABAHÇE PALACE

We enter the filled-in garden
by an ornamental gate
to join an English-speaking
group, patiently queuing
for the grand tour.

We slip disposable,
frilly, lilac-coloured,
plastic bags
over our trainers
as a token of respect.

13 years in the building,
the monoblock covers
45,000 square metres
and cost 5 million
Ottoman gold coins—

equivalent, we learn, to
35 tonnes of gold.
14 tonnes of gold leaf
gild its ceilings,
hastening the bankruptcy

and ultimate collapse
of the Ottoman empire.
Over-reaching himself,
the 31st Sultan tried
to emulate Versailles.

His Armenian architects,
sought to blend eclectic elements—
Baroque, Rococo, Neoclassical
and Ottoman— into a synthesis.
But, lacking taste, they failed.

French baccarat and Czech
Bohemian crystal chandeliers
weighing a ton. A triumphal
staircase, banisters of glass.
Hereke carpets, draperies,

Victorian hangings, opulent
habitats of mites and dust.
Lavish fireplaces. Ornate
parquet floors. Hideous objets
from Europe and the Orient.

We trail through
285 rooms and 43 halls,
studying lilac-coloured shoes.
At any moment, a cobwebby
Miss Havisham may appear.

Imperial decay like a miasma
infests each melancholy room.
Up in Pera, foreign embassies,
smirking behind their hands,
looked down, biding their time.

EBENEZER'S JAUNDICED EYE

This accursèd season of goodwill
makes me ill
from overkill
and, oh by gosh, by God, by golly,
sick of mistletoe and holly.

Although I suspect it would be wrong,
every schmaltzy Christmas song,
each screaming advertising jingle,
genuinely makes me long
to eviscerate Kris Kringle.

EPIPHANY

Gold, frankincense, myrrh—
a bargain exchange rate for
the Light of the World.

ERIC

Schooldays are long gone,
Montpelier, Germany,
Greece, the Lebanon.
I picture him in sunshine,
not that terrible darkness.

ELEGY

The trawlers have gone.
Massive oil support vessels
dominate York Street

which has itself gone,
Victorian tenements,
Dickensian slums

eradicated.
Good riddance. Razed to black earth
that was our playground.

The shipyard has gone
which employed half the city,
or so we believed.

My old school has gone.
Do Fittie kids now study
in a cement works?

And the fishmarket,
with miles of smoot h, hosed-down floor
where I rode my bike.

That was long ago
and in another country,
when I was a boy.

FEAST OF MICHAELMAS

The Feast
of Michaelmas
trumpets the archangels
Michael, Gabriel, Raphael—
all saints.

Because
it coincides
with Harvest Thanksgiving,
it was customary to roast
a goose.

Roast goose
at Michaelmas
was believed to protect
against future economic
downturns.

A ring
found in a pie
at Michaelmas was held
to betoken an imminent
marriage.

No doubt
this would offend
some vegetarian
sceptics and the Health and Safety
brigade.

FEEDING FRENZY

A drake paddles towards me with its head,
spectacularly, iridescent green.
Two dozen cousins foraging for bread,
gliding behind, appear upon the scene,
where peace is palpable this Hallowe'en.

I scatter bits of bap. Immediately,
as out of nowhere, gulls swoop down, a flock
of sharp-beaked gannets, cackling raucously.
Snatching the food in flight, mid-air, they mock
the quiet ones, politely taking stock.

FERGIE

One of the reasons
for coming back when we did,
we missed him by hours,
as we miss his genius
for friendship and his laughter.

FIRST DATE

I brought you a book—
The Story of San Michele—
and wore my long coat,

appropriated
afterwards by Clint Eastwood.
(Spaghetti Westerns

were alien to me,
not my normal habitat.)
And you laughed, blithely.

FIRST LOVE

How sad that cherries
sometimes ripen too early
and that frost blights them.
Sad that the first narcissi
seldom survive beyond March.

FOLLOWING MacCAIG

These are the roots that clutch,
the ferns and fronds that snare
heart, mind, imagination, self-esteem,
that sabotage creativity
and undermine endeavour,
swathed in its plaid of mediocrity.

A giant precedes us up the rocky path,
the long, slow, panting, parallel ascent
adjacent to the whitewater Kirkaig.
In ten league boots, he strides across Assynt.
We Lilliputians, unable to keep up, stumble in his wake
and sink into the peat-bog of his footprints.

We often fall upon his bounty, experiencing largesse,
and pick up nuggets scattered from his horde,
liberated gemstones, precious and semi-precious,
to be collected, fondled , envied and caressed:
cairngorm, carnelian, amethyst and malachite,
snowflake obsidian, chrysoberyl and chalcedony

that scintillate like the river in the gorge,
careering over waterfalls, filling the salmon pools.
Profound and playful, perceptive, witty, wise,
he celebrates a pantheistic holiness.
Lolling on his Parnassus, Suilven,
he puffs his pipe. And smiles, lugubriously.

FLAMENCO

Downstage, a woman
steps into a pool of light
in a long, red dress.

She stands very still,
her body a liquid curve,
a gladiolus.

The music begins,
a soft chorus of clapping.
A strumming guitar

strikes percussive chords.
An old gypsy steps forward,
a ravaged beauty,

unleashing a line
of quavering, high-pitched notes
that resurrect love,

lost love lamented,
now recalled in bitterness.
Even the lemons

know the pain of love.
Milk-white palomas have felt
the heartbreak of loss.

The young dancer stirs,
head held proudly high, back straight
as a foxglove stem.

Growing impatient,
her feet tap a slow rhythm.
Hips sway, arms uncurl,

svelte hands glide like birds.
Blood pulses feverishly.
The thrumming quickens.

The dancer's red skirts
swirl like the wings of a bird,
as she turns and turns

her scented body
to the frenzied rhythm of
the old gypsy's song.

A flower, ablaze,
her scarlet skirts spread like wings.
Her passion reaches

its flurried climax.
Harsh, paroxysmic music
shudders to a halt.

Arms upcurled, lyre-like,
she stands, sweat beading her brow,
back taut as a bow,

her proud breasts heaving.
Abruptly the performers
both turn on their heels

and depart the stage,
in opposite directions,
to roars of 'Olé!'

FOOD CHAIN

A Cape Gannet lands
with executioner's eyes,
ready for battle.
Its breeding grounds are threatened
and it is prepared to die.

FOR SHONA

When you were a child,
you ran races with the wind.
Now it has claimed you.

If you must leave us,
it is fitting you should go
in January

when nature is dead,
the whole world is in mourning
and the sky weeps tears.

FORTINGALL YEW

This venerable yew
was already ancient
when Pontius Pilate,

a Legionnaire's son,
romped beneath it
as a boy.

Its closest contemporaries
are the tortured
olives of Gethsemane.

FROM OUT WASTE PLACES COMES A CRY

The light has gone out
and the house stands in darkness
beneath a black shroud.

Wilderness stretches
far beyond the horizon.
Dawn fails to appear.

The birds are silent,
trembling on cold, dead branches
and the wind laments.

GLOW-WORMS

Lightning bugs wink
their goblin lights
among the grass

like fallen stars.
Pale green radiance
excites our wonder—

the fire-worm's
glimmering tail dipped
in luminous paint.

GREGG'S

La patisserie
of Paris and Amsterdam
is food for the gods.
Consider *les tartes aux pommes.*
Still, we have Gregg's the Baker.

GIVING AND RECEIVING

Giving is blessèd,
for in giving one receives
abundant return.

After the blizzard,
the back garden lay buried
under two foot drifts,

deep, smooth, untrodden
snow as silent as a shroud.
Like an Eskimo

I waded through it,
carrying a sack of seeds
for the bird feeders.

My green wellingtons
sank into virgin quicksand.
Snow spilled into them,

over the boot tops.
With refrigerated toes
and a witch's nose

like an icicle,
fingers frozen to the bone,
I fulfilled my task.

My daily reward?
I celebrate survival,
those who have come through.

Now I'm visited
by miracles, every
colour of the rainbow.

GLORIA IN EXCELSIS

'The world is charged with
the grandeur of God'
Gerard Manley Hopkins

Towards sunset
on a glorious autumn day,
with other pensioners
we clambered aboard
Stagecoach number X59
bound for St Andrew's Square,
and swiped our bus passes.

We had strolled to the Cathedral
and beyond, down to the ancient pier
to watch the rollers breaking upon the rocks,
had pottered around the shops
and lunched well at The Doll's House:
sea bass, green salad and a glass of Chardonnay.
Now we were heading home.

The skies above Fife were vast and shimmering,
cumuli rimmed with scintillating gold.
Then, hallelujah. A sudden epiphany.
The heavens were filled with endless skeins of geese,
a thousand thousand soaring a mile high
above the Eden, arrowing homewards,
murmuring praise.

HAMLET COMPLEX

There must be
a scientific term
for self-doubt.

A hundred yards
into my walk
I ask myself,

did you lock
the front door?
Then go back

to find out.
And, of course,
it is secure,

battened tight, snug
as a bug,
safer than the

Bank of Scotland.
Even the alarm
is set fair.

Three weeks after
sending a cheque
covering my subscription

to Quantum Leap
or The Dilettante,
I ask myself,

Did you really,
or merely intend
to, do so?

The cheque stub
answers the question
to my satisfaction,

that is, until,
with chequebook stowed
in a drawer,

I ask myself,
Did you check
the pesky stub,

or merely intend
to do so
and then forgot?

So with kettles,
gas and electricity,
the heating system

the Potterton boiler:
Did you or did you not
switch them off?

Dressing-gown-swathed
comatose and tousled,
blear of eye,

I lurch downstairs
on naked feet,
challenging my neuroses.

Like Dr Johnson,
I also avoid
stepping on cracks.

HERE COMES THE CAVALRY

Six hundred fat kids in a line queue up
for lunch—reconstituted slurry, lightly heated
spamburgers, turkey twizzlers, Seven Up—
in half an hour the exercise completed.
For 37P, each fat kid's fed,
doubtless to flourish on this low-cost crap
or in their salad days to end up dead
from excess of cholesterol and pap.
But, patience, fat kids. Help is on its way,
designed to trim the waistline of your jeans
as galloping Jamie leads the cavalry,
scattering mangetout, carrots, aubergines.
Let's dedicate this celebratory ballad
to vinegar (balsamic) and green salad.

HERMITAGE

The older I get
the more I keep my front door
locked from the inside.
I like art, books, silences
and traffic passing outside.

HIGHLAND FASHION

A Glaswegian who went to Toulouse
sporting form-hugging, tartan-striped trews,
said , 'Ah'm no really built
tae appear in a kilt
except when emboldened by booze.'

HOBBY

Of all the falcons,
the most elegant killer,
a glider pilot

and sleek assassin,
a swashbuckling, swaggering
dragon-fly-hunting

acrobat, it plucks
swifts and swallows from the air,
plummets and plunges,

shaped like an anchor,
to the depths of destruction
then, exulting, soars.

HORSE CHESTNUT

Stirring
from tight-packed buds,
leaves unfurl and expand,
drawing sap up the fissured trunk.
The force

that makes
the rising sap
quicken to swell the leaves
is one of nature's mysteries,
the fuse

that drives
its hidden power
beyond explanation:
like white candles, the handiwork
of God.

HOORN

Three Dutch boys,
immortalized in bronze,
create a huddle

in the *hafeneck,*
berthed schooners bobbing
beneath the Disneyesque,

Gothic sea-tower,
pinnacled and improbable.
A straggly tree

defies salt winds.
The autumnal sun
signals late October

as drizzle threatens.
Old houses lean
askew over cobblestones.

All three wear
cut-down pants
like pedal-pushers,

rough hempen shirts,
and are shoeless.
One is standing,

thin arms folded.
One leans, slouching
against the wall.

The fat one
in the middle
sits, legs dangling

above a school
of oblivious fish.
Three sea-gazers,

familiar with horizons,
they stare outwards,
out beyond Hoorn,

its anchored barques
with intricate rigging
and lashed canvases,

beyond the immobile
heron, like Jeremiah,
guarding a fo'c'sle,

imagining distant lands—
Tierra del Fuego
and Cape Horn,

Tasmania and Batavia
where their grandfathers
voyaged, trail-blazing.

IF WINTER COMES

A resurrection
recycles last month's blizzards
as seas of snowdrops

studded with islands
of glistening aconites
like hallelujahs.

IN A GRAIN OF SAND

The Summer Exhibition
at the RSA
occupies many rooms

in the classical,
Gothic-columned temple
on Princes Street.

Most memorable work?
A meticulous drawing
of a dragonfly.

IN TESCO'S CAFETERIA

My unaccompanied neighbour
is having breakfast,
khaki Kenco cooling

in unfriendly plastic.
His fried egg
looks distinctly underdone,

his synthetic sausage
a bizarre quadrilateral.
I resist temptation.

IN THE XVIIIth ARRONDISSEMENT

We climb Rue Lepic,
continue up Tholozé.
A lighthouse beckons.
Le Moulin de la Galette
draws Francophile romantics.

IN TORPHINS KIRK

The day thou gavest, Lord, is ended;
the darkness falls at thy behest.
Hearts that are broken must be mended,
griefs and sorrows be redressed.

So little time thou gavest her
to work thy bidding here below,
the joys of motherhood to savour
before the sunset's golden glow.

So fleeting and so few the years
to clasp her objects of devotion
and salvage joys from vanquished tears—
enough to overspill an ocean.

She passed this way and filled earth's byways
with an eternal, heaven-sent light,
illuminating all our highways,
a beacon through the darkest night.

Now thou hast called her home again
to where she rightfully belongs,
to glory far beyond our ken
and radiance hymned in angels' songs.

Acceptance may not be suspended.
Thus we restore her to thy breast.
To thee our morning hymns ascended.
Thy praise shall sanctify our rest.

INTERNET SUGGESTIONS, FATHER'S DAY

Because he forked out all these years for your education
took you on holiday to Butlin's and Bognor Regis
lent you small change whenever you were skint
a shoulder to weep on when you were down
kept you supplied with books and the necessities of life
bought you a comprehensive range of Airfix models
picked you up after school, Scouts, Saturday soccer
let you run carefree through your terrible teens
took you to your first Test Match
organised trips to Alton Towers, the beach, the V & A
put bread on the table and maintained a roof above it
lay anxious and awake in times of vicissitude

Why not name a star after him, a chrysanthemum,
or designate him Lord of the Land?
send him on a trip to Taba Heights, Uzbekistan
or sign him up as a space tourist?
open a subscription in his name to Forbes Magazine
nominate him as a volunteer for Hell's Kitchen
or let Oxfam recycle his plus-fours?
buy an outboard motor for his zimmer frame
a Stannah Stair-lift, a battery-operated comb?
arrange for him to attend a Britney Spears concert
or meet Beyoncé and the Red Hot Chilli Peppers?
introduce him to hang-gliding, swimming with dolphins
or pay for one free-fall parachute jump?
organise a candlelit dinner for two
with a Cabinet Minister of his choice?
send him a ticket for penguin parade at Chessington Zoo?
invite him to pre-select his own de luxe hardwood coffin
from our exclusive internet catalogue range?

IS THERE

any virtue
in using the title
as the first line of your poem?
Like this?

It lends
a small frisson
of immediacy,
spontaneity, of going
straight in.

The new
Scotch Laureate
did so the other day
and it seemed to work very well
for her.

ISAIAH 61

The earth
refreshed by rain
summons forth new green buds.
Flowers spring up in the sun-drenched
garden.

JAPANESE COOKING

Earth, air, water, fire
and the whole world of nature:
Haiku recipes.

JELLYFISH

Delicately beautiful,
snake-haired, translucent
parachutes of gelatine,
blood-red or pallid
blue albinos, they
go with the flow,
drift with the currents,
backwards, forwards,
mindless aliens,
in gang-like shoals.

They don't swim but move
by pulsating water
from pale canopies.
Contemporary, feckless,
passive and lacking
backbones, brains,
ears, eyes, hearts, minds,
souls and ambition, they are
vacuous, their lives
devoid of interest.

JOUST

'I'm a member of Mensa,' he said.
' Many thousands of books have I read.
My amazing I.Q.
means I'm brighter than you.
So piss off, you illiterate ned.'

JOB

Eliphaz, Bildad
and Zophar—Job's comforters—
were self-righteous prigs,
spouting inane platitudes
that completely missed the point.

Elihu, the son
of Barachel the Buzite,
offered raw insights
with the confidence of youth,
further trying his patience.

Exasperated,
he clearly disdained them all.
Abject misery
reinforced his defiance,
buttressed his integrity,

darkened his despair,
added gall to his passion.
He was maltreated
by an adversarial,
unjust, unaccountable,

invisible God,
a morally tarnished judge,
executioner
and abuser of power
who had a bet with Satan.

JUST LIKE DIAMONDS

Swirling in the wind,
accumulations of snow
glisten like spindrift.

KAMCHATKA

In last night's dream I was in Kamchatka,
a thousand miles from the nearest railhead,
at the end of a bleak peninsula,
looking down at floes on the Bering Sea.
No sun. No birds. No animals. No tracks.
No vegetation. No human habitation.
A promontory in a wilderness.
I stood alone, shivering in the cold,
watching the icebergs, far below, drifting by,
like islands disappearing into mist.
How had I reached that place? I do not know.
What was I doing there? I cannot say.
Tongue parched, a cold sweat on my brow,
I suddenly awoke. It was still dark.

LADYBIRD

Call her Carmen.
She is Sevillana,
an Andaluz dancer

swathed in cochineal,
scarlet gown peppered
with full stops.

Everyone adores her
until, wings splitting,
she suddenly skedaddles.

LAKESIDE, CUMBRIA

On a bench
overlooking Rydal Water,
opposite Nab Cottage,

we drink in
the golden extravaganza
of Dora's Field,

beside St Luke's.
No opium eaters
anywhere in sight.

LAST LINE OF DEFENCE

All of life is there,
all of my life at any rate,
clinging to the door of the fridge,
sustained magnetically.

Two denizens of the deep, photographed
in the Oceanographic Museum, Monaco,
signify travel. This one resembles
Ena Sharples. That one, Lord Prescott.

Three snapshots of our grandson, Max,
gaze back at me through frank, observant,
sceptical, twelve-month eyes. He rations smiles
and weighs things up, deliberately.

In the garden my three sons grin at the camera
against a backdrop of geraniums and rhubarb.
Handsome. All different. All alike.
I helped to make them.

Their bonny wives are smiles personified,
strangers who chose to join the family.
Who would have dreamt in starting out
the world would shrink to one vast triangle?

A quadrilateral of magnets
conveying memories through cherished images.
The Kitchen Maid. A Degas Dancer. The Garden of Earthly Delights.
Two magnificent Van Eycks and four Van Goghs.

A scattering of vowels and consonants
at Max height from the floor.
He likes to play with them, lifting them on and off,
learning to permutate words.

And, at the centre of this small collage,
outside the Begijnhof in Bruges,
or leaning against the tomb of Bishop Elphinstone,
you, held by magnets, as my last line of defence.

LAST OF THE LIBEN LARKS

Africa's prodigious,
magnificent and vast,
large enough to guarantee
its ecosystems last.

Notwithstanding, the Liben lark
is destined shortly for the dark.
Environmentalists don't hold out hope
for this obscure songster, an Ethiop.

With fewer than a hundred left
the continent will be bereft
of this sweet, diminutive songbird's chirrup,
mellifluous as golden syrup.

It won't be seen near any zinnia
in Somaliland or Abyssinia.
First African bird in recorded history
to go extinct. Quite the ornithological mystery.

It won't be found perched on a cactus.
Its terrible silence may not impact us.
But when the last of them drops dead,
spare a thought for mankind instead.

LEAVING THE NEST

They left,
London calling,
bright lights of the West End,
three hundred miles of Motorway
ahead.

I stood
at the front gate,
waving my handkerchief,
voicing an unspoken prayer.
But why?

He is
now the same age
as I was when I drove
from Scotland to the Lebanon
and back.

He has
a new SatNav,
a valid MOT,
AA membership and a map.
They'll be

OK
despite the frost,
the inadequacy
of the A1, the explosion
of cars

and trucks
on the highway
since you and I set out.
And, besides, they will be back on
Friday.

LEIDEN

We went by train to Leiden,
hoping to see the Rembrandthuis,
the Korenbeursbrug over the Niuwe Rijn,
the ethereal tombstone of the 15th Century merchant,
Floris van Boschhuysen and his wife,
standing, like Adam and Eve,
in naked bas relief,
inside the Pieterskerk,
the ancient, venerable University
and other miscellaneous antiquities.

Instead, we took in the Jazz Festival
in the Railway Station concourse—
a dozen moustachio'd old boys on the side of life,
in bow ties, fancy shades and striped gilets,
rocking the rails with *Basin Street Blues*
and *It Don't Mean a Thing if it Aint Got That Swing.*
Contemporaries of Cab Calloway and Jack Teagarden,
their average age was 80-plus.
Later, we ate battered, deep-fried fish
from a polystyrene tray beside the Botermarkt.

LOBSTER

Antennae waving,
a drowning crustacean
squealing in the pot.

LOBSTERS AND LOCUSTS

Solitary, subaqueous lobsters
crawling across rocky sea-beds,
prospecting vitrified ocean floors
in their fine blue shells,

and county-sized swarms
of grasshopper–green locusts,
descending in ravening clouds
to denude fields of hard-won maize,

share a common etymology:
Old English *lopustre,*
cognate with Latin *locusta.*
Both are armoured, segmented predators.

Dropped into boiling water,
the lobster's deep, metallic blue turns scarlet
with chagrin or embarrassment. On moveable stalks,
its swivelling eyes weep tears, turn blank with grief.

The clawed lobster in its scarlet carapace
occasionally appears in still-life paintings
as a surrogate for the devil. Yet it is noble,
handsome, long-lived and delicious.

Locusts arrive like clouds of dust
stripping the African landscape bare.
Individually insignificant,
they are wastrels, jumping out of the way,

but, in the mass, devourers, pestilential as the plague.
They wreak vast destruction. Deep blue, scarlet or
emerald green, lobsters and locusts eat, and are eaten,
in times of abundance, in times of austerity.

LOVELACE

Broken in health,
confronting adversity on
the losing side,

reduced to rags
in obscure backwaters,
the laughing cavalier

carried on laughing
with defeated friends,
tankard in hand.

LUGWORM

Pink or black in its narrow grave
inches below the surface of the sand,
king-lug, the gulley worm, beds down,
beloved of godwits, avocets and fishermen.
Between its silty, untidy worm-cast
like a Walnut Whip, and two concentric circles
dimpling the sand a foot away as targets,
perfect spheres from an RAF fuselage,
its sepulchre is easy to identify.
The resurrectionists have it easy.
All that is needed is a broad-tined fork,
a bucket of clean saltwater, for rinsing,
and a pail, for portability. Six decades ago, my Dad
and I, mackerel-men, played Burke and Hare.

LUNAR ECLIPSE

I slipped out of bed
and through the bedroom window
looked out at snowdrifts.
Would flights delayed from Heathrow
make it to Scotland today?

In the dawn moonlight,
the park was cold, white, silent,
archipelagic
as an alien gulag.
Huddled birds. Crystalline trees.

At six this morning,
the full moon shone like silver,
illuminating
a world transformed, in the week
of our Lord's nativity.

Then its glowing face
was covered by a shadow
that obscured its light
and threatened its radiance.
Its luminosity dimmed.

By seven, darkness
had created emptiness
and a sense of loss.
The bright-faced moon had gone out.
Birds in the gulag shivered.

LUNAR OBSERVATION

The pinnace sails on.
Just two, he gazes upwards.
It glides between clouds.
'The moon is hiding,' he says.
'It's hiding behind the trees.'

MAGIC CARPET

Crocuses create
a springtime kaleidoscope,
yellow, white, purple,
a carpet from Bokhara,
emblazoning the landscape.

MASTER WORKS

What do atheists
feel when confronted by faith
that is palpable?

Michelangelo's
masterpiece required ten years.
Handel's just three weeks.

They were both inspired
by what atheists deny:
the glory of God.

MARRAKESH

A suicide bomb
has destroyed the balcony
where we sipped mint tea.

ME AND MY SHADOW

My doppelgānger is a hobgoblin.
I glimpse him lurking in the neighbour room,
forever watching me when I come in.
Constant attention makes me fret and fume.
Sometimes I chance upon him unawares
impertinently gazing through the glass.
He observes me running up and down the stairs
and sniggers cynically as I pass.
Unlike myself, young, spry and debonair,
he's elderly, arthritic, manky, grey,
suffering from gout and paucity of hair.
His erstwhile joie de vivre has ebbed away.
I struggle to ignore him. Is it rude
to be offended by his snide decrepitude?

METAMORPHOSIS

A swallow flies south
from the Garden of England,
heading towards France.
Halfway across the Channel
it becomes a hirondelle.

ME SHELLEY, YOU JANE

Once in Cavite—
a novice scuba diver—
the current was strong.
I swam down to the sea bed
waiting for my Dive Master

but he never came.
The fact that I am writing
this little poem
after my lonesome sojourn
points to a happy ending.

Once in Boracay
when a long, black water-snake
zig-zagged towards you,
you fast-crawled back to the boat,
an Olympic champion.

MONYMUSK RELIQUARY

This embossed, peaked thing
of wood, silver and copper,
the *Breac Bannoch,*

containing relics
of the saintly Columba,
inspired the armies

that it preceded
into battle—like the Ark
of the Covenant.

MEMORIES

I recall
squeezing brambles
through a pudding cloth
tied to two brush handles
how one winter
the Dee froze over
and bus stops
were sepulchred
in snow-drifts
five feet deep
the one hour stopover
at the Kingsway ice rink
in Dundee
half-way to Edinburgh.

Christ's view
of the favelas
from the summit
of Pan de Azucar
a virgin-white hilltop
and dappled ice-cold tree-trunks
in San Carlos de Bariloche
the savour of alabalik
of grilled trout gathered
from an Anatolian waterfall
bamboo-tied
prayer-flags
addressing the wind
above Bhutan.

MILLER'S TALE

Heavy-hearted Priscilla Miller
spotted a hairy caterpillar
a wriggling, multi-limbed, brown cedilla
crawling around a vestigial pillar
on the tropical island of Anguilla
to which it had sailed from remote Manila
in a rackety Mindanao flotilla
commanded by a slit-eyed killer,
a degenerate maritime guerrilla,
with emery skin like Polyfilla.
He spun the wheel and worked the tiller.

The hirsute, frolicsome caterpillar,
fur-coated as a small chinchilla,
had nibbled a leaf of granadilla
green salad garnished with cascarilla,
masticating with strong maxilla.
It took several sips of sarsaparilla
flavoured with cinnamon and vanilla
with a hint of gluten-free manzanilla,
some tropical hardwood its distiller.
The name of this wriggling grub? Attila,
whose partner went by the name of Scylla.

Priscilla that day was distinctly fraught,
fractious, crabby and overwrought.
Her love-life had withered away to naught
with the loss of her beloved consort,
missing in space, an astronaut,
revolving like an afterthought.

The tropic sun was too fierce and hot
for siesta-ing on her davenport
or for forty winks on her bedroom cot.
Causing her cheekbones to distort,
it turned her complexion apricot.

It cooled a little towards nightfall.
Protected by her parasol,
she sauntered over a leafy knoll
aware that the sun had begun to fall
as nightingales commenced their call,
holding her burdened heart in thrall.
She watched the caterpillar crawl
over a stump, a hirsute ball
performing a version of rock and roll.
Emitting a plaintive caterwaul,
she squashed it against the garden wall.

Atilla, my son, were you not aware
as you wriggled and writhed beneath nut-brown hair
that it would have been wise to stay well apart
from this woman grieving with heavy heart
as she set out on her evening stroll
rather than bug her with rock and roll?

MODERN CRUSADERS

We flew in yesterday
from Scotland
via Heathrow,
crowded as ever
with nowhere to sit down.

You flew in today
from Indonesia
via Singapore
and the artificial birdsong
of Changi Airport.

Skirting the Sea of Marmara
and following the ancient crenellations,
taxis brought us to our hotel in Pera
where, reunited, we now sit
breakfasting on waffles and maple syrup.

NOVEMBER FIRST

The moon, till recently a perfect sphere,
is now a silver crescent in the sky
which this November morning arches clear,
crisp, blue and virtually cloudlessly
between horizons, like a symphony.

The year will shortly sink down to its core.
Wildfowl will huddle in the frozen grass
and leafless trees stand desolate and hoar.
High in the stratosphere two aircraft pass
inscribing on the heavens a Christian cross.

MORE THAN GOLD

Love unqualified,
without frontier or limit,
is worth fighting for,
overcoming all constraints,
wading through Hell to achieve.

Unconditional
love that knows no boundaries,
absolute, total,
is the desired objective,
the wished-for consummation,

the sure foundation,
the alpha and omega,
be-all and end-all,
quintessence of fulfilment.
Life's high mead. The Holy Grail.

ON PLANTING DAFFODILS

Golden-headed dancers
almost invariably disappoint.
These fifty bulbs,

planted in expectation,
will provide gratification
for three weeks

in early Spring
before degenerating into
dishevelled, unkempt slatterns.

MUSCLE TONE

Soldiers
of Christ arise
and put your armour on.
Take up your breastplate, sword and shield.
The

language
of religion
is metaphorical
and sometimes the analogies
may

appear
literal and
obscure, causing offence.
It may be more acceptable,
now-

adays
to consider
religion as akin
to a journey or sea-voyage—
not

at all
as a crusade,
with its connotations
of conflict and hostility.
All

the same,
I like the sound
of breastplates and armour,
and of a robust, muscular
faith.

NOTES FROM 1964

I remember
her love for her Dad,
graduate of Ellis Island,
a multilingual carpenter,
dead before we met.

Recall
her love for her Mom,
American archetype
with a heart of gold,
defender of the world's flotsam,
whose lemon meringue pie was to die for.

Her shy entry,
like a de-hibernating dormouse
or irresolute crab,
into that first cocktail party,
the intellectual turbine-room
and glittering demi-monde
of Almagro cinco.

Her passion for all things Spanish:
paella and the Prado,
Don Quixote de la Mancha,
chocolate con churros,
the Sierra de Guadarrama,
Las Casas Colgadas,
el Cieglo d'Oro,
the Alhambra.

Her carrier bag,
full of holiday snaps
of a student trip
in a crowded Volkswagen Beetle
around the classical sites
of Europe:
Slavonic donkeys,
Italian chickens,
Peloponnesian sheep and goats.

I remember
the laughter
and spontaneity
of a dark-eyed child
with an I.Q.
in the upper stratosphere.

And recall,
fondly,
with a smile,
her figure-flattering ski pants
and matching,blue,
bum-hugging anorak.

OLDER THAN THE ROCKS

Mona Lisa's granddad,
I sit expectantly
at the concert

of Valentine Favourites,
scanning the programme.
Christian Vasquez, Venezuelan

Conductor: twenty seven.
Alice Sara Ott,
German-Japanese pianist:

just twenty two.
The orchestra consists
predominantly of teenyboppers.

Even more sobering
is the fact
that tonight's acclaimed,

international composers—Tchaikovsky,
Rachmaninov, Mahler, Ravel—
died, mere fledglings.

OUTLOOK

In the Lothians,
skies are traditional grey.
Rain and wind prevail.
But the sun will emerge soon
and turn the harvest to gold.

OLIVES, GRAPES, CICADAS, SUN

Groves of olive trees
spell Mediterranean,
their native birthplace
festooned with Doric temples.
Homer is their husbandman.

Grapes hang from the vine,
purple, black, yellow, green, pink,
drinking in the sun.
Twinned with olive trees, grapevines
triggered civilization.

Clicking and buzzing,
cicadas vibrate tymbals
in their abdomens.
They produce, bouzouki-like,
the music of Ancient Greece.

Glorious Apollo
shines down upon vines and groves,
sheep, goats, oracles.
Where cicadas create choirs,
columns stand bathed in sunlight.

PEACH

A peach's future
depends on its core, the stone
nestling at its heart.

ON READING BURNTISLAND BLUES

With your Mum and Dad,
you travelled to Burntisland
for beach holidays,
renting a tenement room
in a Somerville Street flat.

With my Mum and Dad
I went from Somerville Street
to Edinburgh
holidays in Auntie Kate's
flat at 18, Buccleuch Place.

We took vacations
on either side of the Forth,
twenty miles apart,
you looking southwards at me,
I looking northwards at you.

Had I known you then
we might have arranged something—
either a house swap
or an exchange of poems,
celebrating poverty.

Burntisland Blues by Jim C Wilson, *The Oldie,* November 2010.

OVER THE WALL

My young friend, Leo,
likes to keep me company
when I mow the lawn.
He will be four next birthday
and views my work-in-progress

from the garden wall.
We have a sealed agreement
that when he is ten
and I'm a hundred and five,
he will cut the grass for me.

PADDLING TO EL DORADO

The Forth
and Clyde Canal
links two mighty oceans.
From Musselburgh you can reach
New York.

Sit tight
in your kayak
when you get to Falkirk.
Archimedes' screw will hoik you
on high—

better
than climbing stairs.
The only problem? Draft.
The canal is not terribly
profound.

PETÉN

The howler monkeys
roared nearby. We were relieved
they weren't panthers.

POLITICIAN, LAGOS

His amber eyeballs,
reamed with suggestions of blood,
betoken evil.

His feral henchmen,
on the brink of anarchy,
employ machetes.

QUIETUS

The finality
of death is unbearable,
yet it must be borne.
Here today. Gone tomorrow.
the truism that all must face.

RAIL BRIDGE

Humps loom through Scotch mist
drifting like cotton candy
above the Forth.
The bridge appears sinister—
a visitor from Loch Ness.

PRAYER FOR JAPAN

After multiple catastrophes
and despite vast
loss of life,

a waste land,
sodden and broken,
an impenetrable future,

Biblical tribulations, dread
of the unknown,
their spirit endures,

undemonstrative, unbowed, remarkable.
Despite crippling shortages—
food, water, petrol—

they maintain order,
civic and personal,
decline to brawl,

whinge, rant, shove
or ransack supermarkets.
Crossing erstwhile streets,

they patiently await
the green man.
Cocooned in grief,

no one sounds
his car horn.
Gaman is paramount,

patience, resilience, stoicism.
Dear Stoic God,
succour singularity, collectively.

PROGNOSIS

Of the type, you volunteered,
they consider progressive.
Ostensibly under control,
it may recur at any time,
in any part of the body.

I stood at the window
overlooking the canal,
considering the ramifications,
weighing up the pros and cons
of anxiety and distress.

Return to work? Doubtless
unfeasible. And Kurdestan?
No doubt off limits. Never again
to comb long, lustrous hair.
How will the grieving family fare?

And as I stood, on the canal,
the surface choppy from the freshening wind,
there glided past a solitary swan,
veeing triumphantly towards the east,
pushing aside the waters with its breast,

to where the sun will rise tomorrow
to dry our tears and wipe away our sorrow.

RAISE ACCLAIM

Raise your eyes from the ground. Embrace the rays
of the sun in enfolding arms.
Salute the firmament.
Hail the oceans.
Acclaim
the miracles
of earth, sea, sky and birth.
Worship the lamb. Welcome the child.
Raise your sights and rejoice in the sun's rays.

REÁL COLEGIO DE L'ASUNCIÓN

Five decades ago
when the world was young,
life was for living.
There were songs to be sung.

I walked into a classroom,
and met my future wife.
That day I won first prize
in the lottery of life.

RECESSIVE GENES

Like little lobsters,
they often hide
under large stones

or in burrows
in the banks
of big rivers.

Crayfish, disturbed, escape
by shooting backwards
into second childhood.

RECYCLING

At night,
(old wives' tales claim),
whenever they are parched,
spiders suck moisture from your lips
and eyes.

Later,
ravening worms
move in and have a feast,
not unlike a Jacobean
banquet.

REJUVENATION

Through an incision
in my wrist, a catheter
like a tapeworm snakes

up my arm, across
my thorax into my heart
and has a look-see,

reconnoitring
a narrowing artery.
Blow up a balloon:

party time is nigh.
After I've been inflated,
fitted with a stent

and made young again,
I shall dance an eightsome reel
in celebration--

joined by Prof. Newby
and his team, in a circle,
led by Jimmy Shand.

RESURRECTION

Blind,
she will not see it
or be able to visualize
what it resembles.

Deaf,
she will not hear it
nor recognize the welcoming bells,
the susurration of angels' wings.

Senile,
incontinent, confused,
her mind far gone,
inhabiting a twilight zone,

she will have no recollection
of what lay around her
in her infancy, of how
the Old Masters depicted it

in paint, music, poetry,
or retain the faintest memory
of home, hospice and her ultimate,
walnut-scented journey.

Asleep at last,
all suffering past,
to oblivion are consigned the tears,
kindnesses and unstinting love
that sustained her throughout so many years
and now accompany her above.

RETURNING TO BYZANTIUM

Borne by an eagle,
we survey two continents
and the Golden Horn.

Beneath lies Europe,
ahead of us Asia
criss-crossed by bridges

and an armada
of ferry-boats. Merchantmen
doze through siesta

peacefully, anchored
in the Sea of Marmara,
enjoying the sun.

There's the Bosphorus,
those dots the Princes Islands.
The channel arrows

through to the Black Sea,
pathway to the Crimea,
Samarkand, Tashkent.

Istanbul has spread
in the past forty five years
since our honeymoon,

the Vauxhall Viva
heading into the unknown.
We did not get lost.

Some things have not changed.
Down there's the Galata Bridge,
with men still fishing

for hybrid sardines
from conglomerate waters.
For *ekmekbalik.*

RITE OF SPRING

God knows where
in outer darkness
they have been

this past sixmonth
of relative silence.
They are back

on chimney pots,
composing Spring symphonies
with golden nibs.

ROSE WINDOW

Refracted at Chartres,
red and gold sunbeams scatter
the grandeur of God.

What are we doing
about reflecting the light
that shines through stained glass?

ROBIN

I stand with my key
poised to open the front door.
Snow lies all around,

silent as a shroud.
Then materializing
as if from thin air,

just two feet away
on the encrusted railing,
a redbreast alights,

black eyes glittering.
It cocks its head to one side,
inquisitively,

becomes a fluff ball,
feathers challenging the chill,
and asks: 'Where's the bread?

I rather suspect,
were I to invite it in,
it would hop inside,

perch on the TV
or on a shelf hung with cups
to enjoy the warmth.

In our all-white world,
the red smear of the bird's breast
restores me to life.

ROYAL WEDDING

Flowering cherry
flutters down like confetti,
appropriately.
Springtime has done its research
on pathetic fallacy.

A glorious day
of national rejoicing.
Camped out on the Mall,
we can forget our troubles
and the enemies within.

RYDER CUP

The heavens opened
and Welsh monsoons
inundated the course.

Wide Sargasso seas
covered the fairways,
greens waxed tidal,

mudbound marquees sagged.
Then glory dawned,
warming a continent.

SAD

Darkness at dawn.
Darkness at noon.
Darkness at dusk.

Unsleeping, I lie
in the half-light,
relentless Scotch rain

cauterizing the tiles,
a November gale
attacking the foundations.

I stare blankly
through a tunnel
arrowing into winter,

the entrance huge,
the exit tiny
and far distant.

Perhaps within it
we shall circle
the dark drain,

unclogged by leaves
that fell recently,
spilling their gold.

The black hole
will grab us
as we swirl

round and round,
sucking us down
into its maw.

SANDAKAN

The orang-utans
assembled at a set time
for their tea-party,
swinging from the canopy
like ladies from Cheltenham.

SCAN

We study the scanned
x-ray image that you brought
for us to inspect,

trying to make out
recognizable features,
nose, fingers, toes, smile,

but it is too soon
to discern resemblances.
She is at this stage

a mere radar blip,
an electro-magnetic
smudge, reflecting love.

SCARLET & BLACK

Rowans hang blood-red
against the river's blackness,
hang like drops of blood
against the dark mystery
of deep, black, fathomless pools.

SCHISMATICS

So many churches
undergoing conversion
like new Dissenters.

Knox advocated
a school in every parish.
The Victorians

held similar views
about church building. Holy
Corner's well endowed.

City centres fade
as suburbia expands.
Congregations die.

These brave Gothic piles
now house gambling casinos,
furniture show rooms,

experimental,
Fringe theatres, youth hostels,
Pilates courses,

repositories
for fitted kitchens, yoga
and linoleum.

SERENDIPITOUS IN FLORENCE

Apart from
digging up
Maris Pipers
in the Spring,
and scooping virgin
white rotundities
from nurturing loam,
there are few pleasures
greater than turning
from the hot and heaving,
traffic-heavy streets
into a dark, refreshing church

and finding, unexpectedly,
in a tenebrous, cool apse
or on a shadowy wall,
some Quattrocento
masterpiece or other,
a Nativity or Crucifixion
scene, a Massacre
of the Innocents by
a long-dead master,
lurking, like buried treasure.
Insert a coin, and let
illumination flow.

SHONA

She sparkled, Feugh-like,
reflecting summer sunlight
that perfumes the breeze.
Water carried her laughter
over pebbles to the sea.

SIMPLIFIED HISTORY

Bosworth Field. Richard,
pleading in vain for a horse,
settled for a hearse.

SKYLARK

Like a symphony
it soars towards the heavens
trailing songs of praise.

SLEEP ON, ARCHDEACON

Few enthusiasts read
Barbour's *'The Brus',*
a long, vernacular,

mediaeval Scots romance.
The Twin Towers
of St Machar's

perpetuate his memory.
Over six centuries,
this is noteworthy.

SLOE DRIZZLE

Sloe gin is not laborious, but slow—
(patience, but no cooking required.)
Prick the blackthorn berries
with a clean pin.
Drizzle
caster sugar.
Store in a dark cellar.
Shake weekly for two months. Dark red,
sloe gin is like nectar. Savour it slo-o-o-o-o-w.

SNOW FALL

Cars like Christmas cakes
under a foot of icing
without marzipan.

SOUTH WEST 19

Friday, 1st July.
Above the Pentlands,
cotton-wool cumuli

congregate like whales
in the stratosphere,
cavorting in pods.

Rain showers loom,
long, dark shadows
threatening SW19.

SMALL

I sit
at a small desk
in a minuscule house
not dissimilar to all its
neighbours.

The town
in which I sit,
clutching my ball-point pen,
is no vast megalopolis
but big

enough
to meet my needs.
My country is minute,
a petite punctuation-mark.
If viewed

from space
it must appear—
if at all—as a dot,
a poor, undernourished comma
that God,

doubtless,
scarcely perceives
through His binoculars.
The planet which I occupy
is S

not M,
L or XL.
its solar system but
one of an infinite series.
In view

of this
immensity,
I question the purpose
of sitting here clutching my pen,
scratching

away
in the darkness,
ask, what does it avail
to confront insignificance?
Don't you?

SPIDER AND FLY

Spinning
a dazzling web
into which you entice
lunch is sinister and scarcely
cricket.

ST ANDREW'S CATHEDRAL

The cackle of gulls
has for centuries proclaimed
the inheritors.

STAND-UP

Your thought-processes
lack propriety, finesse,
a sense of fitness.
You are a mediaeval
mocker of dwarves and cripples.

Your gutter language,
though typical, still insults
the land of your birth.
You offend your audience
of lemmings, plus those at home

who can exercise
their annihilation rights
by switching you off.
I rise to my feet, sighing,
and consign you to darkness.

Why make jokes (?) about
an eight year old, handicapped,
blind, brain-damaged child
who has never caused you harm
and has no right of reply?

Can't you imagine
him, in his wheelchair, captive
in darkness, not in the park,
playing football with his pals?
Smirk, you shark-skinned blasphemer.

I do not know him
or any other victim
fixed in your cross-hairs.
But I can give him a voice
and bombard you with tankas.

You bully. You thug.
You pathetic Glaswegian
inadequacy.
How did our mountain torrents
and glens spawn the likes of you?

The world is drowning
in a swamp of nastiness.
Do not add to it.
Your cutting-edge, avant garde
humour(?), lacking kindness, stinks.

SUN AND SONG

Sunlight,
strained through stained glass,
scatters a bright rainbow
over the nave's mediaeval
flagstones.

Articulate
songbirds
in sycamores and elms
fill Princes Street Gardens with hymns
of praise.

STEADY AS A ROCK

Fourscore quiet years
devoted to family,
church, the Women's Guild,
life in a granite city.
Her heart hardened. Then she died.

STILL LIFE WITH FLAT CAP AND PIPE

I wear my Dad's cap
which my mind's eye sees him in.
It fits precisely.
And I cherish your Dad's pipe
which I never saw him smoke.

SWALLOWS

Circus performers,
belly-skimming the river,
sipping surfaces

without getting wet,
they rid the sky of midges,
mop up mosquitoes.

Hawking for insects,
they dive bomb with precision,
like trapeze artists.

STRAIT IS THE GATE

The pathway to God
is seldom easy
or straightforward.

For the baptism,
we had to get
to Coldstream Kirk,
thirty-odd miles away.

That Sunday morning,
there was a blizzard,
an arctic whiteout
hurling driven snow
against our windscreen,
horizontally.

We could not see
the windfarm's
ghostly blades,
revolving slowly
above Lauder.
The highway
was devoid of cars.

Towards Carfraemill,
even before we reached
the long, slow haul up Soutra,
we decided to turn back,
considering it wiser
to abort than to proceed.

Using our mobile phone,
we called the Minister,
explained our problem,
expressed our disappointment,
and apologised
for any inconvenience caused.

She listened sympathetically,
with palpable concern,
said that it would be foolhardy
to continue and urged us
to drive home cautiously,
taking the utmost care.

Within an hour
of our arrival,
she called us back.
If we could drive
to Eddleston—just
fifteen miles away,
with no significant
gradients to negotiate—
she had the key
to the village kirk
and would be happy
to conduct the baptism there.
How about 3 o'clock?
Was that convenient?

Arrangements made,
we met her there

in the bare, unheated,
empty, little church,
snow-garlanded,
all five of us in overcoats,
thick scarves
and woollen gloves.

We stood around the font
like early Christians
in a hidden room
or secret cave,
for all the world
like ancient Thessalonians
or new Corinthians.
Her words and living breath
rose up like incense.

Afterwards,
she locked the door
behind her, carefully.
We walked into a Christmas
card of robins, holly,
virgin drifts
and icicles depending
from the eaves.

Hugely exhilarated ,
we slithered down the hill
for further sustenance
at the Horseshoe Inn.

SUILVEN

Viewed
from the icy fjords of The Minch
by Vikings marauding down the coast,
its seaward profile is a column of rock.
Its name in Norse
is Pillar Mountain.

Viewed
from the metropolis of Lochinver,
across the sea loch
and beyond Glencanisp Forest,
it is magnificent, improbable,
a dour, surrealistic, snow-besprinkled
but unsweetened Sugar Loaf,
a policeman's helmet carved in stone.

Viewed
from the north or south,
across peat bogs and lochan-strewn wilderness,
it is a recumbent pachyderm,
a slumbering mammoth with a noticeable waist,
lolling apart
from its siblings in the herd:
Canisp, Quinag, Cul Mor, Stac Pollaidh and Cul Beag.
Of all of these
it is the greatest and most magnificent.

And yet, surprisingly,
for all its fearsomeness,
Suilven's summit is benign:
viewed
from the cairn,
a field of gently-sloping grass,
a football pitch,
besprinkled with heather and clusters of edelweiss.

SUPPER AT EMMAUS

You can go
to the New Testament,
to the apostles, Luke and Mark,
for narratives of the encounter,
some threescore furlongs from Jerusalem,
with supper at Emmaus afterwards.
Neither Cleopas nor his companion
recognised their Lord, the risen Christ.
Only when he broke bread were their eyes opened.
Then he vanished away.

You can go to London,
to the National Gallery, and study Caravaggio.
His great chiaroscuro depicts a beardless Jesus
appearing to the astonished Cleopas
and awe-struck, gesticulating Luke,
a pilgrim's scallop shell in his lapel, arms outstretched
in his extreme bewilderment, as at a crucifixion.
All eyes are fixed on Christ.
Bread and wine are on the table. Apples, grapes, pomegranates
tremble on the edge. The ichthyotic shadow of a fish.

Or you can go to the Holy Land,
taking care to avoid bombs and bullets, gunfire and grenades.
From Jerusalem, set off walking along the Emmaus road
in sunshine perfumed with olives, lemons, pomegranates,
and heady with birdsong.
Take bread, grapes, a wine-flask
and your New Testament.
After some threescore furlongs, rest on a wayside mile-stone.
The beardless stranger you encounter
will gladly share your journey.

TAKING STOCK

Waxing furious
at something we must have done,
He won't be appeased
by prayer or sacrifice,
suffering or contrition—

the rape of the earth,
the pursuit of evil, sin's
glorification,
the building of Gomorrah,
the worship of false idols.

Penance is futile
before His terrible rage
has blown itself out.
Boats are tossed up on the shore,
drought decimates the forests,

floods engulf Queensland
and the Amazon dwindles
to a foetid stream.
Deserts usurp our vineyards
and dead fish rot in the sun.

Let us build an ark,
of gopher wood, robustly,
and with our loved ones
set sail upon the waters
in search of a green landfall.

TAKING OFF

Before matins
in the Cathedral
of Burgos,
I heard
the mouse-like
pittering of nuns
crossing the Plaza
in the half-light.
I rose to watch them
from the hotel window.

Their cornettes
were like white sails
of Spanish galleons,
the wings of doves,
preparing to soar.
Heading for Madrid
and the New World,
I, too, was ready
to take off, on the brink
of something new.

THE LONG GOODBYE

After the shortbread,
we waved farewell, not dreaming
it was for ever.

THE JOY OF SEX

Females of more than eighty species
feast upon their lovers
during or after sexual intercourse.
Witness the praying mantis

which, *in flagrante*, takes peculiar delight
in tearing off its beloved's head
then devouring the rest of him
leaving (possibly) just the wings.

Stag fights with rutting stag, true monarchs
of the glen, until both drip blood
and the defeated one bows out,
crestfallen, with flayed antlers.

Glaswegian-style, uxorious walruses
and love-lorn sea-lions
slash with their canines
at each others' throats.

Porcupines drench potential mates
with urine, while the female hippo
faces a fragrant and unforgettable offering of
far-flung faeces.

Stick insects are obliged
to copulate, uninterruptedly,
for ten whole weeks. Lady millipedes
spit on their eggs, just for the hell of it.

And female green spoon worms
inhale their mates—insignificant motes of dust
200,000 times smaller than themselves—
like pinches of snuff.

Animals are brutish, violent,
profligate and promiscuous in their coition,
forever releasing clouds of gametes into the sea
or entrapping multiple mates to ensure fertilisation.

I much prefer human romantic sensibility
which associates love with the music of Mahler,
the poetry of Burns, Byron, Pushkin and Neruda,
and a dozen pints of Newcastle Brown Ale.

THE DECEIVER

A halcyon morning.
Above the surface
of the stream

streaked lightning skims
low, a fragmentary
flash of paradise,

like a rainbow.
With harpoon beak,
it tastes foul.

THE TREE OF LIFE

The cosmos shudders. Galaxies explode.
Eruptions spew forth red hot magma. Seas
attack the rocks, engulfing continents.
Foul hellbroth bubbles at the earthquake's core.
An infant's foot, cupped in a mother's hand,
is as a prayer, a psalm, an act of worship.
A butterfly lands, trembling, on her wrist.
Sunflowers turn golden faces to the sun
and giant redwoods soar towards the sky.
The eternal river burbles over stones.
With arms upraised, clutching his father's hands,
a twelvemonth child steps out into the world,
its future strewn with suffering and loss,
and beauty scattered everywhere, like balm.

THROUGH THE SCENT OF WATER

After months of storms,
property values collapsed
amid ice, snow, hail.

Our fuchsia bush
succumbed to the conditions,
like its successor.

What is to be done?
Why, we shall emulate Job,
dig in, start afresh

and set out new pots
filled with red geraniums
to flourish next June.

TRIBUTE

Heaven is no single place
but is ubiquitous,
surrounding us with tenderness
wherever we may be:
in Cheam, the Drakensberg, Old Aberdeen,
Chicago, Wengen, Grindelwald,
Castel Gondolfo, Banchory,
in Trastevere or on Deeside,
when leaves cascade from alder trees
and naked rowans shiver in the mist.

O, she excelled at everything she turned to.
potholing, softball (representing the Transvaal),
golf, tennis, skiing, rowing, squash.
She was a springbok, a gazelle,
a love-child of the wind,
downplaying her abilities,
always magnanimous in victory,
for ever gracious in defeat.
She hurdled over two degrees,
started to make her mark upon the world

but found her true vocation in her son,
in motherhood, in developing the young.
Her genius was for nurture and creation,
her youthful work-in-progress moulded
in her image. Like hers, his smile
invariably lights up the room.
Her legacy to him is one of laughter,
kindness, gentleness, transparency
and fearlessness in tackling adult slopes.
Cruelly bereft, he is the child of love,

personifying resurrection. For resurrection
is a living memory, a praising and rejoicing,
a work well done and seen to be well done,
a memory that survives. Experience does not die
but lives on, everlastingly. Pain, sorrow, suffering,
weakness, death are but essential parts of life,
precursors to ensuing victory. Heaven is no single time,
but it is every time, within time and beyond time,
where love endures all and forgives all.
Heaven lies all around us, ubiquitous and eternal.

TURKISH DELIGHT

At Topkapi Saray,
we look askance
on those reprobates,

Selim the Sot,
Ibrahim the Crazy,
and similar unworthies.

With shining eyes,
we'd rather contemplate
Roxelana the Beautiful.

TO EVERY LEAF A SEASON

There is a beauty
in trees
in each and every season
of the year.
Month by month
throughout the turning year
trees are a recurrent
miracle.

A springtime beauty
in fledgling larches,
beech trees, elms,
when delicate fresh young leaves
burst forth from the darling buds of May
like gossamer bright green butterflies
bursting free
from the cocoon of winter.

A beauty
in July's languorous foliage,
gloriously swaying
when winnowing summer breezes
create adagios
from drowsiness and torpor
and rustle up symphonic
tone poems.

A beauty
in September's alchemy
converting
the green of oak, ash, birch
and sycamore into sublimest gold,
or staining them scarlet,
blood-coloured,
hectic red.

A wintry beauty
when December's fang
strips branches to the pith,
and falls of snow
form Chinese masterpieces
of filigree and lace,
when Brueghel picks out black silhouettes
against the pale light of the dying year.

TRAILING CLOUDS OF GLORY

We didn't visit Muncaster Castle
which friends advised us was extremely nice,
our diffidence not premised upon hassle,
disinclination not based on ticket price.
Likewise on the Aquarium we chose to pass,
opting to save it for a rainy day.
We left the cod, the cuttlefish, the wrasse,
and, turning down a C-road, slipped away.
We're rather fond of dawdling out-of-doors,
among the crags and tarns, the coombes and ghylls,
and scrambling over hows like herbivores,
identifying with crowds of daffodils.
Not wishing to seem ungrateful or unkind,
we prefer fells and waterfalls and wind.

TRIP ADVISOR

A glorious vista,
especially at sunset
on declining days,

studded with jewels,
the skyline of Istanbul
takes away the breath.

Magnificent mosques
with minarets like lances
control the seaways.

Aya Sofya,
Sultan Ahmet, the Yeni,
Suleimaniye,

a score of others
sharing Topkapi's bounty
between continents.

But the Chora Church,
pride of Edirnekapi,
is our favourite.

Ancient, separate,
away from the madding crowd,
dignified, it stands

in a little square
far removed from the hubbub
of tourist footfall.

Enter the low door,
into the vaulted arches,
plain, modest, naïve.

Eyes turn heavenwards.
The frescoes and mosaics
are testimony

to an age-old faith,
enduring for centuries,
captivating souls.

ULLAPOOL, AFTER RAIN

We cross Kessock Bridge
and take the Road to the Isles.
A shaft of sunlight
strikes gold—Bethlehem nestling
at the end of the rainbow.

UNDER THE LAGOON

Forests felled in Istria
and Illyria shore up
the Adriatic pearl's
corrupt foundations.

Every so often
they must be replaced
to prevent the jewel's
decaying into slime.

UP AND DOWN

From Tibidabo,
we looked upon Middle Earth
stretched out before us.

At Corcovado,
we stood at the feet of Christ
and surveyed the world.

ULTRASOUND SCAN

After the Atkins Diet of lean steak and green salad,
and, for breakfast, a surprisingly Full English,
without milk or carbohydrates,
I proceed clinic-wards, blood pressure rising
at the paucity of parking, to encourage 'bus travel.
Walking into the wind is difficult.
Simply to stand upright is difficult.

Medical forms. Medicinal chat . A recent prescription
as Exhibit A. Height. Weight. Blood test.
A plastic cannula like a leech sucking the crimson essence.
Injection of a special tracer.
Then ninety agreeable minutes on a metal bed,
in an antiseptic room, a soulless, walled-in narrow box,
alone with Albert Camus and *The Adulterous Woman,*
joyless, in their Algerian wilderness.

For the ultrasound, they load me like a torpedo
into a bomb tube, an ancient, man-size embryo
reverting to the womb. A gentle whirr. Thrumming,
I glide towards nirvana, reassured that the state-of-the-art,
Siemens PET CT echo scanner is German-made, a guarantee
of longevity. (Witness our freezer, twenty-year-old Braun mixer,
ancient electric knife.) It's siesta time.

Eyes closed, hands clasped behind my head, knees gently raised,
I lie there like a mediaeval effigy, drifting across a featureless
expanse
of drab Maghreb, of unrelieved North African scrub.
No palm trees, water or alleviating dunes, no wadi or oasis
on this side of the horizon. Merely moraines of stone,
grey stone dust everywhere, rasping and cold, testing the eyeballs,
with, bleak among the stones,
dry grasses, brittle stalks of straw.

UPWARDS

Contented in the Newby Bridge Hotel
we take our ease after our Lakeland day,
swooping from Kirkstone Pass to Morecambe Bay,
taking in crowds of daffodils as well.
We tackled Aira Force and Cartmel Fell.
The track around Tarn Hows was kiddie's play.
Wordsworth and family graced our matinée
with Dora's Field a golden bagatelle.
We can no longer climb the Langdale Pikes,
or tackle the ascent to Watendlath,
the days long gone of youth hostels and bikes.
Dinner over, beside this cosy hearth
we sit contented after gentle hikes,
a game of Upwards and a soothing bath.

UPSETTING THE APPLE-CART

Butch, unmarried, in her mid-forties,
the hatchet-faced policewoman
was having a bad day, distemper
and disenchantment etched on her face.

She insisted on inspecting the fruit-seller's
vendor's licence, which he did not have.
Unable to comply and impotent, he whined,
prevaricated. She tipped over his handcart,

scattering in the gutter his pathetic horde
of clementines and apples. Inflamed
with fury, gorge rising to choke him,
he remonstrated verbally, shouting abuse

at this woman, this dog, this daughter of Eve.
She slapped his face, there in the medina,
surrounded by traders and bruised, fallen fruit,
his apples and pomegranates festering in the filth.

From an adjacent stall he snatched a plastic,
paraffin-filled container, and muttering imprecations,
oaths in the name of Allah, charged across the square,
to the gendarmerie. Only to be met with ridicule,

indifference, contempt. Slouched in their chairs,
the enemy blew smoke rings, answering his complaints
with snickering obscenities, guffaws. A black mist rose.
A stiletto pierced his soul. He poured the paraffin

over his heart and limbs, then struck a match,
a blow for martyrdom. Self-immolation sparked the fire
that ran like a contagion through the country,
then grew and grew into a general funeral pyre.

VAGABOND

Like swallows seeking winter sun,
we flew south to escape the cold,
the frozen tundra and ice fields
of Novaya Zemlya.

From our bedroom window
in the Hotel Suisse,
nestling beneath the castle rock
and the tomb of Garibaldi,

we looked out over a blustery sweep of bay
held in an all-encompassing embrace,
the sickle of the Promenade des Anglais,
in the old year's dying days.

Shingle chill beneath naked feet,
not even the Germans were queuing for a dip.
A Dufy chorus line of palms like *midinettes*
coquetted around the shore towards Antibes,

beyond the Hotel Negresco
and le Musée des Beaux Arts.
Immediately in front of us a public garden
no larger than a pocket-handkerchief.

Our nearest neighbour occupied a bench
from which, for seven days and nights,
as far as we could testify, he did not budge,
except, presumably, to pee. For which we cannot vouch .

Bearded like Santa Claus, he wore an Inca hood,
at least three coats plus several layers of indeterminate,
unspeakable bin bags. On his feet, king-size sneakers
beneath a veritable barbican of socks.

He was Falstaffian in his bulkiness
and, in his general immobility, statuesque.
Around the bench, like votive offerings,
a dozen plastic bags held all his worldly goods.

Five-decked pleasure palaces jostle in marinas
all along the Azure Coast. Cruisers from Guernsey
and the Cayman Islands, with sun decks
from the Ritz and the Savoy, for Happy Hour.

Beneath the traffic lights, shrouded in plastic bags
he sat, all day, all night. Occasionally les flics appeared,
rolled down their window, proffered digestive biscuits.
The lights changed constantly, disrupting sleep.

How must it feel to dwell among the sybarites
to have no walls, nowhere to wash,
no bed and almost no belongings,
no fire, no fuel, no friends, no family?

On our last day, as a near neighbour,
I crossed the road and introduced myself.
gave him some Euros, and wished him 'Bonne Année.'
We shook hands formally. He wished me 'Meilleurs voeux.'

Beyond the Negresco lies the airport of the Côte d'Azur,
behind which loom the snow-clad Southern Alps.
Lights change from red to green and back again to red.
Months have now passed . I expect he has not moved.

VALE OF TEARS

La Niña drags the Pacific towards
Australia. Bolstering clouds, it falls as rain.
Mighty rivers, Fitzroy, Burnett, Condamine, Ballone,
rampage through Rockhampton and Toowoomba.

Less powerful than September's 7.1
but only three miles down, the quake stikes close to home,
at lunchtime. Christchurch at its busiest.
The spire collapses. Ten thousand homes face demolition.

Tectonic plates collide beneath the sea,
setting off cataclysms. Tsunamis follow,
obliterating bullet trains and whole communities.
Japan sucks in its breath , awaiting meltdown.

The world lurches on its axis. There is nothing
to be done, but to endure. Silvery-tinged,
my love's becoming short of breath, a little deaf.
I take her hand in mine, and hold it tight.

VIRGILIAN VESPAS

At Sigiriya,
irate hornets attacked us
beside the frescoes,
buzzing like demented bees
disturbed in their siesta.

But give them their due.
As we slalomed and abseiled
in panicky flight
down that helter-skelter rock,
the malcontents did not sting.

VENUS

The morning star shines
gloriously in the sky,
just before daybreak.

VISTA

Venetian blinds
cannot keep out radiance.
Our guest house window
affords a panorama
of twenty formative years.

WHAT WILL SURVIVE

With our bus passes
we travelled to Dunfermline
and the Abbot's House

for lunch in the sun,
yesterday's Royal Wedding
still resonating

with the happiness
that united all of us.
Larkin's words ring true.

WAITING FOR DAWN

Prostrate with grief, perhaps,
or grieving with prostate,
I lie awake, awaiting daybreak.
Broken-backed, I greet the dawn.

I greet the dawn,
drowsing, greet it
at least four times
before the rising of the sun.

I lie awake, listing the countries
we have visited, alphabetically.
I list their capitals. I draw up lists
of alphabetic rivers, endlessly flowing.

Aardvark to zebra, I list the animals,
fishes and birds, avocet to yellowhammer,
a cross between Funk and Wagnell
and St Francis of Assisi.

I construct short verses in my head,
haiku, tanka, sijo, doggerel.
All, by dawn, will have evaporated,
like morning mist.

I have no rosary, no worry beads
but say The Lord's Prayer umpteen times
in silence, to myself, hoping my loved ones
will survive the rising of the sun.

WALKING BACK TO BABYLON

An old woman and her grandson
trail for miles across the surface
of the moon, a desolate expanse
of parched wilderness devoid of trees,
vegetation, water, hope.

Barrenness surrounds them,
It extends to far-off horizons.
Nothing life-affirming except the boy
and his wooden, shepherd's pipe, which he plays
enthusiastically, eliciting fractured sounds.

Blustery siroccos raise blinding dust storms.
Grit and sand assault their eyeballs,
spinifex and tumbleweed like barbed wire
impede their progress.
The granny bows her veiled head:

God is great.
They are journeying to a prison
in the south, seeking a son, a father
missing these many years, a war casualty,
a prisoner, possibly.

Trucks, tractors, buses provide haphazard transport.
An alien language.
They pass crumbling tells and ziggurats,
Beit Ibrahim, Ur, burnt, ruined villages,
a shrunken river, clogged with silt,

and evidences everywhere of mass graves.
In green fatigues, masked men
investigate, calibrate, measure, record,
stuff plastic bags. Black-clad rookeries
of widows ululate into the wind.

WE'D KILLED

We'd cleared the borders of every weed
known to Botanical Science,
napalmed dandelions,
scarified lawns,
killed
swarms of greenfly,
crew-cut privet hedges,
but could not rest on our laurels.
We'd been had. The resilience of the weed!

WEED KILLER

The hour hand revolves
and days are dropping like flies
with nothing achieved.
In the interstices, weeds
cluster and choke the driveway.

Irresolution
akin to paralysis
holds me in its thrall.
Docken and dandelion
spread their stubborn pestilence.

What is to be done?
I shall utilise napalm
in a bombardment.
I shall mount an offensive
and zap those loathsome taproots.

WEEKEND BREAKS

Constantinople
and the Byzantine Empire
are splendiferous,

Aya Sofya
and the Sultan Ahmet Mosque
truly breathtaking,

Topkapi Palace,
spread on its promontory,
a source of wonder.

Crowning waterways,
one of the world's great skylines
completes the sunset.

We go sub-surface.
In Justinian's cistern,
carp hover like ghosts

around Medusa heads.
Dank Mesquita arches rise
out of still waters.

In comparison,
Newby Bridge and Ullapool
are a tad smaller,

less populated,
not strategically key,
bi-continental,

imperial powers
embodying centuries
of ancient culture.

But we love the Lakes
with the April daffodils
celebrating Spring,

and the Summer Isles
dozing peacefully offshore,
just beyond Assynt.

WHEEL OF FORTUNE

A spinster from Lytham St Annes
was just one of life's drab also-rans
till her number came up
in the Cheltenham Gold Cup.
Now the Vicar is crying the banns.

WHEN ICICLES HANG BY THE WALL

Allosaurus-shaped
teeth hang like a portcullis
from dripwater rones.
Rows of spiky stalactites
brandish armouries of spears.

WINTER FEEDERS

Mistle thrush, fieldfare,
redwing, goldcrest, willow tit,
tree creeper, starling,
house sparrow, brambling, siskin
gather in a found tanka.

WINTER LANDSCAPE

Through the mist
come the shouts
of excited children

on red sledges
worshipping the snow.
They are mesmerised

by the fact
that the world
has been transformed.

I can hear
but cannot see
their Brueghelian games.

On plastic trays
they hurtle down
snow-covered slopes

that at Eastertime
serve equally for
egg-rolling competitions.

Along both banks
of the canal,
like Chinese lithographs,

delicate water-colours
of filigree tracery,
their branches cradling

virgin white offerings,
the trees shiver
in shrouded nakedness.

The rotund belly
of the sonsy
snowman, towering above

untrodden playing fields
is patriotically swathed
in a Saltire.

Whatever its origins,
this snow man's
an avowed Nationalist.

WITHOUT PRICE

Our first grand-daughter,
curled quietly in the dark,
arrives this summer.
The pearl of the Orient
will eliminate Scotch mist.

WORDS OF COMFORT

He invoked glory,
peace, redemption, grace,
freedom from bitterness,

caritas, going before,
waiting for others,
our coming afterwards.

Peace? Unglimpsed. Unlikely.
Glory? Impossible abstraction.
Bitterness? Scalding tears.

WORLD WITHOUT END

Drops of falling rain,
turning parched pastures to green,
are uncountable.

The sands of the sea
cannot be calculated.
They are infinite.

The wisdom of God,
wider than oceans and skies,
knows no horizons.

Without bound or end,
the days of eternity
will last for ever.

YOSHINO AND FIRE

Not trees but events,
milestones in the calendar,
yearly cult objects.
Like Magi, pilgrims journey
from afar to worship them.

Japanese cherries
erupt in pink explosions
on Fujiyama
while Egyptian flame trees,
turn the streets of Cairo red.

ZOCODOVER PLAZA

A cold country of oppressive heat,
with, at its core, the endless plateau
of La Mancha, burnt umber by last summer's sun,
el hogar de los pobres,
wearing today a turquoise canopy.

The Imperial City of Three Cultures
stands on a plate that tilts towards the river,
looping around it in a deeply incised gorge:
the former capital more ancient and more venerable
than the recent upstart, with its room for growth.

If you are fortunate, you may walk down, as we walked down,
one fine, serene, crisp, January morning
towards the Tajo from the Parador. Walked down
into the gorge, to enter the city, as if for the first time,
on that glorious first morning of the year,

broom glistening with dew, a sufficient sun
warming our backs. Across the gorge's rushing river,
the city scrambles up the slope, a jumble of red roofs,
stone towers and crooked lanes with, dominating all,
the stark Alcazar and the cathedral's spiky spire.

The entrance to this labyrinth of intricate passageways?
Ignore the new bridge used by motor cars. Continue
to the old Alcantara with its high stone arch,
its horseshoe gate and flight of zigzag steps
mounting the city's rocky, mediaeval flanks.

Go past the Hospital de Santa Cruz, climb up
another flight of steps, pass through a second horseshoe gate,
the Arch of Blood, to reach Zocodover, still echoing
from the siege of the Alcazar, looming adjacent.
In this triangle beats Toledo's heart.

Here you may rest from your exertions
in the January sun, and join the Toledans sitting
where they have always sat, beneath umbrellas.
A dish of hot tortilla, crusty bread, a caña of ice-cold beer:
manna with which to consecrate the day.

ZODIAC

Earth, air, fire
and water dominate.
Arrows, claws, horns

and hooves prevail.
But Scorpio crawls
on the ground,

hypnotizing the twins
with the sting
in its tail.

Indigo Dreams Publishing
132, Hinckley Road
Stoney Stanton
Leicestershire
LE9 4LN
www.indigodreams.co.uk

Papers used by Indigo Dreams are recyclable products made from wood grown in sustainable forests following the guidance of the Forest Stewardship Council.